MANIPULATION BODY LANGUAGE DARK PSYCHOLOGY

The Ultimate Guide to Influencing People Through Persuasion Techniques, Mind Control & Emotional Manipulation

By

Robert Meyer

Table of Contents

INTRODUCTION

It's a safe assumption that you've been with someone on a date and thought to yourself, "I really like them, but what do they think about me?" When you are interested in someone, it can be a nagging question, and you really hope that the feeling is mutual, but without coming right out into the open and asking, you have no way of knowing. To do this, very few people have the nerve. Most people have heard of romantic body language, but there is no clue about how to read and interpret it for the vast majority of the population. It is a very real thing, and knowing how to read the signals that are relayed to you by the other person can quite often make the difference between getting a second date or missing out on a potential relationship. If you want to sniff out signs that a guy likes you (or vice versa, of course), becoming a fluent reader of one's body's suggestive movements can help you notice every tiny little subtlety that the individual sends in your direction unconsciously. In a number of different ways, romantic body language can be displayed, including things like eye contact, body gestures, and the way a person speaks. If you know what to find and how to look for it, in a short period of time, you can become an expert and know the answers to any of the questions you have about a specific individual.

This book will explain how to make the differences evaporate by manipulation. Without the messiness of conflict, manipulation is about getting someone to submit. Lying by omission is manipulation.

"I want you to think of me better, so I won't tell you this secret." Secrets in a relationship are often small deaths. Secrets avoid vulnerability.

Secrets readily pile up over time for too many couples. Many couples are awful at speaking about difficult things, and deflection is the norm. Piling up silent resentments instead of struggling with honest dialogue can be very manipulative. It's really a way to manipulate the argument that "if you really love me, you would know what I want and how I feel." It's a belief that avoids the responsibility and vulnerability of asking for what you want. It's your task to make yourself known, no one else's. Manipulation, instead of negotiation, demands obedience. True dialogue is erased by manipulation. Manipulation requires people to be either right or wrong, and no shades of gray are allowed. Manipulation kills relationship growth because honest conflict does not have room. In this book, you will learn the techniques to manage manipulators and avoid being manipulated.

In this book, you will also know how to identify and avoid being a victim of manipulators, predators and emotional manipulators in a relationship.

CHAPTER ONE

DARK PSYCHOLOGY

Dark Psychology is both a construct of human consciousness and a study of the human condition as it relates to people's psychological nature to prey on others motivated by psychopathic, deviant or psychopathological criminal drives that lack instinctual drives, evolutionary biology and theory of social sciences in purpose and general assumptions. Humanity, as a whole, has the potential to victimize humans and other living beings. While many sublimate or restrain this tendency, some act upon these impulses. Dark Psychology investigates the minds of criminals, deviants, and cybercriminals.

Dark Psychology is the general study of the human condition as it relates to the psychological nature of individuals motivated by criminal and/or deviant drives that lack purpose and general assumptions of instinctual drives and the theory of social science to exploit other individuals. In order to victimize other people and living creatures, all of humanity has this potential. At the same time, this tendency is restrained or sublimated by many, some act upon these impulses.

Dark Psychology seeks to know those thoughts, feelings, perceptions and systems of subjective processing that lead to predatory behavior that is antithetical to human behavior's contemporary understandings. Dark Psychology assumes that 99.99 percent of the time, criminal, deviant and abusive behaviors are deliberate and have some rational, goal-oriented motivation. It is the remaining .01 percent, part of the Adlerian theory and the Teleology of Dark Psychology. Within the human psyche, Dark Psychology postulates that there is a region that allows some people to commit atrocious acts without purpose. In this theory, the Dark Singularity has been coined.

Dark Psychology claims that without any coherent rationality, all mankind has a store of noxious purpose towards others, going from insignificantly prominent and short lived musings to unadulterated psychopathic degenerate practices. This is called the Continuum of the Dark. What Dark Psychology calls the Dark Factor is the mitigating factors that act as accelerants and/or attractants to approach the Dark Singularity, and where the heinous actions of a person fall on the Dark Continuum. Brief introductions are shown below to these concepts. Dark Psychology is a concept that has been grappled with by this author for fifteen years. It was only recently that the definition, philosophy and psychological aspect of the human condition were finally conceptualized.

Dark Psychology covers everything that makes us who we are in relation to the dark side of ourselves. There is this proverbial cancer in all cultures, all faiths and all humanity. There is a side lurking within us from the moment we are born until the time of death, all that some have called evil, and others have defined as criminal, deviant, and pathological. A third philosophical construct is introduced by Dark Psychology, which views these behaviors as distinct from religious dogmas and theories of modern social science.

Some individuals commit these acts and do so not for money, power, sex, retribution or any other known purpose, Dark Psychology postulates. Without a target, they commit these horrid acts. Their ends, simplified, do not justify their means. For the sake of doing so, some individuals violate and injure others. This potential is within all of us. The region that this author explores is a possibility to harm others without cause, explanation, or purpose. Dark Psychology assumes that it is incredibly complex and even more difficult to define this dark potential.

Dark Psychology assumes that we all have the potential for predator behaviors, and our thoughts, feelings and perceptions have access to this potential. We all have this potential, as you will read throughout this manuscript, but only a few of us act upon it. At one time or the other, all of us had thoughts and feelings of wanting to behave brutally. We all had thoughts of wanting to severely hurt others without mercy. You will have to agree that you have had thoughts and feelings of wanting to commit heinous acts if you are honest with yourself.

Given the fact that we consider ourselves to be a benevolent species, we would like to believe that these thoughts and feelings are non-existent. Sadly, we all have these thoughts, and, fortunately, we never act upon them. Dark Psychology suggests that there are individuals who have the same thoughts, emotions, and perceptions but act on them in premeditated or impulsive ways. The obvious distinction is that they act upon them, while others simply have fleeting thoughts and emotions to do so.

Dark Psychology claims that this style of predator is deliberate and has some rational, objective-oriented motivation. Religion, philosophy, psychology, and other dogmas tried to define Dark Psychology cogently. Most human behavior is indeed purposeful and goal-oriented, related to evil actions, but Dark Psychology assumes that there is an area where purposeful behavior and goal-oriented motivation appear to become nebulous. There is a continuum of victimization of Dark Psychology, ranging without any obvious rationality or purpose from thoughts to pure psychopathic deviance. The Dark Continuum, this continuum, helps to conceptualize the Dark Psychology philosophy.

Dark Psychology analyzes that part of the human psyche and universal human condition that makes predatory behavior possible and may even be impelled by it. In many instances, its lack of obvious rational motivation, its universality and its lack of predictability are some characteristics of this behavioral tendency. This universal human condition is assumed by Dark Psychology to be different or an extension of evolution. Let us look at some of evolution's very basic tenets. First, consider that we have evolved from other animals and are currently the model of all animal life. Our frontal lobe allowed us to become creatures of the apex. Let us now assume that being apex creatures does not remove us from our animal instincts and predatory nature entirely.

If you subscribe to evolution, assuming this is true, then you think all behavior relates to three primary instincts. The three primary human drives are sex, aggression, and the instinctual drive to self-sustain. Evolution follows the principles of survival of the species' fittest and replication. We behave in a way to procreate and survive, together with all other life forms. To mark our area, protect our territory and ultimately gaining the right to procreate, aggression takes place. It sounds rational, but in the purest sense, it is no longer part of the human condition.

Our power of perception and thought has made us both the species' apex and the apex of the brutal practice. This writer is certain that you cringe and feel sorrow for the antelope ripped to shreds by a pride of lions if you have ever watched a nature documentary. The purpose of violence, although brutal and unfortunate, suits the evolutionary model of self-preservation. For food, which is necessary for survival, the lions kill. Male animals, at times, fight to the death for the ritual of territory or the will to power. All these acts, violent and brutal, are explained by evolution.

They often stalk and kill the weakest, youngest or females of the group when animals are hunting. Although this truth sounds psychopathic, the explanation for their chosen prey is to decrease their own risk of injury or death. In this way, all animal life acts and behaves. The theory of evolution, natural selection and drive for survival and reproduction relate to all their brutal, violent and bloody actions. We, humans, are the ones who own what Dark Psychology is trying to explore.

When we look at the human condition, theories of evolution, natural selection and animal instincts, and their theoretical tenets, appear to dissolve. We are the only beings on the face of the earth who, without the reason of procreation for the survival of the species, prey upon each other. Humans are the only creatures that, for inexplicable motivations, prey on others. Dark Psychology analyzes that part of the human psyche and universal human condition that makes predatory behavior possible and may even be impelled by it. Dark Psychology assumes that there is something intrapsychic that affects and is anti-evolutionary in our actions. For reasons other than food, survival, territory or procreation, we are the only species that will murder each other.

Philosophers and ecclesiastical writers have attempted to explain this phenomenon over the centuries. We will delve into some historical interpretations of human behavior that are malicious. Only we humans, with a complete lack of obvious rational motivation, can harm others. Dark Psychology assumes that, because we are human, there is a part of us that feels dark and vicious behaviors.

This place or realm in all of our beings, as you will read, is universal. There is no group of people now, before, or in the future walking the face of the earth who do not possess this dark side. Dark Psychology believes that reason and logical rationality are lacking in this facet of the human condition. It is part of us, and no known explanation exists.

Dark Psychology also assumes that this dark side is unpredictable. Unpredictable in the understanding of who is acting on these dangerous impulses, and even more unpredictable in the length of time, some will be totally denied their sense of mercy. There are people who commits murder, rape, torture, and rape without cause or purpose. Dark Psychology talks to these actions of acting as a predator seeking human prey without clearly defined purposes. As human beings, we are incredibly dangerous to ourselves and to every other living creature. The reasons for this are many, and Dark Psychology is trying to explore these dangerous elements.

The purpose of the researcher is to evaluate the nature of Dark Psychology and to understand the origin and development of psychological phenomena that motivate human beings to exhibit predatory behavior in the absence of any apparent rational motivator. This writer realizes that his attempt to succeed in this is almost impossible but hopes that Dark Psychology will cultivate an interest in additional exploration.

We've all got a dark side. It is a factor of the human condition, but it has been agreed not to be well understood. An unpleasant reality, Dark Psychology, surrounds us patiently waiting to pounce. As this writer has already mentioned, Dark Psychology encompasses all forms of cruel and violent behavior. We just need to look at the senseless cruelty of animals. Being a dedicated pet lover, this writer's animal abuse is both vicious and psychotic. As recent studies have suggested, animal abuse combines with a higher probability of committing violence against humanity.

On the simpler side of the Dark Continuum, there is vandalism of other properties or an increasing level of violence in video games that children and adolescents are pleading for during the holiday season. Vandalism and the child's need to play violent video games are mild compared to overt violence, but they are explicit examples of this universal human feature of the author's theory. The vast majority of humanity disagrees and hides its presence, but the elements of Dark Psychology still lurk softly under the surface of all of us.

It is universal, and it is universal throughout society. Some religions say it as an actual entity that they call Satan. Some cultures believe in the existence of evil creatures as being guilty of malicious acts. Dark Psychology has been defined by the brightest of many cultures as a psychiatric condition or as a result of genetic traits passed down from generation to generation.

This researcher attempts to examine the origin and nature of Dark Psychology in order to understand how the average, well-socialized person can end up in the news, having committed atrocious acts that no one could have predicted. At any point of the day and the whole night, since the beginning of the recorded history, the atrocities committed by one human being to another have been unending. Though macabre, it's amazing how apparently decent people could possibly participate in or allow such horrors to occur.

Thousands of these atrocities have been evident throughout history. The holocaust in the Second World War and the ethnic cleansing currently taking place in neighboring countries are just a few examples. History, with the remaining of what Dark Psychology has caused, is full of examples. Dark Psychology, as described above, is alive and well and requires a serious investigation. As you continue to check and explore the tenets and foundations of Dark Psychology, the cognitive framework of understanding will slowly develop.

Understanding Psychological Manipulation

Psychological manipulation is simply a type of social influence that seeks to change the behavior or perception of others through indirect, deceptive, or underhanded techniques. By advancing the excitement of the manipulator, often at another's expense, such processes could be considered exploitative and devious.

Social influence is not necessarily a negative influence. People like friends, family, and doctors, for example, can try to persuade people to change clearly unhelpful habits and behaviors. Social influence is perceived to be harmless if it respects the right of the affected to accept or reject it and is not unduly coercive. Social influence may constitute underhanded manipulation, depending on the context and motivations.

Dark Continuum

The Dark Continuum is an essential element to understand in your passage through the dark side of mankind. The Dark Continuum is simply an imaginary conceptual line or a concentric circle that all criminal, violent, deviant and sadistic behaviors fall. The Dark Continuum consists of thoughts, feelings, perceptions, and actions experienced and/or committed by human beings. The continuum ranges from calm to severe and from objective to aimless.

Obviously, the physical manifestations of Dark Psychology fall to the right of the Dark Continuum and are more serious. Psychological manifestations of Dark Psychology lie on the left side of the continuum but can be just as destructive as physical acts. The Dark Continuum is not really a scale of severity, ranging from bad to worse, but defines the types of victimization in the thoughts and actions involved.

Dark Factor

The Dark Factor is portrayed as the domain, spot and likely that exists in each one of us and is essential for the human condition. This process and concept are one of the more abstract terms of Dark Psychology because it is so difficult to illustrate through written expression. According to the online dictionary, the Factor is anything that contributes causally to the outcome, i.e., a number of factors have determined the outcome. This writer will try to extrapolate to you in a cogent way how Dark Factor resembles an equation.

The Dark Factor is not really a mathematical equation but a theoretical equation. Dark Factor is a set of actions and events that a person experiences, which increases their likelihood of engaging in predatory behavior. Although research has suggested that children who develop in abusive households become abusers themselves, this doesn't imply that all manhandled kids grow up to become savage wrongdoers.This is just one facet of a multitude of experiences and circumstances that contribute to the Dark Factor.

The number of elements involved in the Dark Factor equation is large. It is not the number of elements that cause the Dark Factor to become extreme, but the impact these experiences have on the subjective processing of a person makes the Dark Factor dangerous. Some of these aspects include genetics, family dynamics, emotional intelligence, peer acceptance, subjective processing, developmental milestones and experiences.

Dark Singularity

Dark singularity is a theoretical concept and procedure similar to the definition of singularity in the center of a black hole. When this writer attempts to describe and illustrate the concept of Dark Singularity, he uses astronomy and cosmology as a metaphor to describe that concept. The theory indicates that the singularity is so dense and powerful that the modern laws of physics become entangled in their mathematical equations.

The black hole is the vast expanse of space surrounding the singularity, and the dense light cannot escape it. At the focal point of all galaxies known, is an all-powerful black hole with an infinitely small singularity at its center full of awesome energy. Dark singularity, as in the case of Dark Psychology, is the absolute center of the Dark Psychology universe. Simply put, the Dark Singularity is made up of pristine evil and unduly pure malevolence. The Dark Singularity is the farthest to the right of the Dark Continuum. The person closest to the Dark Singularity is an advanced & severe psychiatrist who victimizes others with minimal motivation or purpose for his actions.

Through the studies of this writer, he grasped many of Adler's theories. To this day, this writer interprets his realm as defined by Alfred Adler, this great physician and psychologist. Adler had many descriptions of human behavior, and this writer integrated many of them during his construction of Dark Psychology. The three most valuable concepts for the development of Adler's theory are as follows.

Adler believed that all behavior was objective. From the moment we are born and come to the earth to the day we leave and die, everything we think, feel and do has its purpose. Nothing that we have started during our lifetime happens haphazardly. Although his philosophy may initially sound simple, it is actually quite complex. In view of this, the motivation behind why people are considerate is that it serves that individual to be so on the grounds that they receive the benefits of being acknowledged by their companions, friends and family and the community.

Children taught to be kind, caring and contributing have a higher level of acceptance of feeling and being part of a group. For Adler, the purpose of healthy functional behavior was to feel part of or a strong need for acceptance by others. Taking his theory that all behavior is aimed at the opposite end of the spectrum, malevolent behavior also serves a purpose.

Adler argued that people who behave in hostile or non-acceptable ways respond to a deep sense of inferiority. When people perceive that they are not part of or not accepted by a social group, they move in a negative direction. As they move further from their innate purpose of being part of social construction, they move further away from treating others with kindness, regard, respect and dignity. Under this tenet, Dark Psychology predicts that 99.99 percent of all behavior is objective. Like Freud and Jung, Adler has subscribed to the philosophy of teleology.

Moreover, as human beings are increasingly discouraged, isolated, and their social environment is increasingly fragmented, the more they lash out to others in volatile ways. The narcissistic psychiatrist would be a prime example and a quick illustration. The narcissistic psychiatrist is unbelievably selfish, finds pleasure in victimizing others, and deliberately takes advantage of others without remorse. The concept of objective behavior is of paramount importance to the understanding of Dark Psychology.

As mentioned above, this writer strongly believes that all human behavior is 99.99 percent objective. The left one is where Adler differs. This is.01% Dark Singularity. Of all Adler's theories, the assumption of all behavior as a goal, is fundamental to understanding Dark Psychology however shifts marginally in the most serious type of pernicious human behavior(s).

The second theoretical tenet of Adler, which is central to Dark Psychology, is the concept of subjective processing. We all have thoughts, feelings and actions that influence the behavior of cognitions and affective states. Conversely, a person's behavior affects his or her cognitions and emotions. Defined as a system or what Adler defines as a constellation, the triad or trinity of human experience consists of an orbiting system of thoughts, feelings and behaviors. Adler has added subjective processing to this human experience system.

He believed that childhood experiences, family dynamics, birth order positioning, the dynamics of inferiority vs. superiority worked in such a way as to create a person's perceptual experience and the trajectory of interacting with his world.

The easiest way to understand the subjective processing and the perceptual framework is to visualize a pair of sunglasses. Your eyes represent reality, and the sunglasses represent your mechanism that distorts the reality of the harsh sunlight. As a result, your "perceptual sunglasses" filter and alter how you can interpret information and respond accordingly.

This is how subjective processing works, but it is applied to the human condition. Reality exists and happens every moment around us. Subjective processing filters our reality, both in order to protect and protect us from what we feel may be countersigned to our objective objectives. If a human develops in an environment where he perceives himself to be part of, belonging to, and accepted, his subjective filtering process enables much more accurate input. He socializes in what he sees as a discouraging environment; his subjective treatment is distorted and confused with selfishness and narcissism.

As far as Dark Psychology is concerned, the aim is to assume that all people filter their world by means of subjective processing. Those people who are violent, aggressive or abusive wear a couple of proverbial sunglasses that are myopic and blurred. These people perceive that others are out to harm them and move to assault or manipulate them first. Their subjective treatment distorts their common sense of dignity, charity and selflessness. Acts of kindness become foreign experiences or are used to manipulate their social environment, guided by a selfish modus operandi.

The third key to understanding Dark Psychology is Adler's Social Interest Theory. Social interest, postulated by Adler, is the combination of perceptions, thoughts, and feelings translated into benevolent behavior. Simply stated, the more a person feels accepted by others, the more they feel part of it, and the higher sense of belonging is directly linked to the social interest of a person. People of high social interest are inherently kind, selfless, giving, and receptive. All these qualities of social interest further strengthen their subjective approach in order to be positive and compassionate. High Social Interest is equal to the low impact of Dark Psychology.

Given that, we all possess a Dark Factor within us; a person of high social interest keeps his Dark Factor subdued. The lower the Social Interest, the more likely the Dark Factor is to manifest. At the point when an individual feels less encouraged, doesn't encounter a feeling of acknowledgment,does not experience a sense of acceptance and sees his reality as disconnection, he is at higher risk of experiencing dysfunctional, hostile reactions. Related to Purposive Behavior,

Subjective Processing and Social Interest are central to the understanding of Dark Psychology.

Dark Psychology is a theoretical design made up of a compilation of the philosophic tenets of Alfred Adler, Carl Jung, the author's clinical experience as a psychologist, his academic and professional experience as a forensic/criminal psychologist, and many years of discussions with his loved ones and colleagues on deviant behavior.

As mentioned earlier in this manuscript, this writer aims to take 15 years of thought and observation and to translate it for others to investigate. The second and most important goal is the hope to defeat those who walk through life looking to harm, victimize, and brutalize.

Others postulate a completely different tenet that is not psychiatric but defined as depletion of conscience. This writer does not spend much time in clinical studies or academic explanations, given the vast amount of work compiled by those studying deviant behavior. The approach is to lay out a wide net to cover the relevant theories that this writer feels are valuable in understanding Dark Psychology.

A portion of the information needed to understanding Dark Psychology is an overview of child development, family dynamics and other factors working to formalize Dark Psychology. Although there is no way to define exactly why and how some people turn to the dark side, there are areas that help explain how the "laws of probability" exist in the development of the antisocial personality construction. Other areas discussed include psychiatric issues, personality disorders and alcohol and drug addiction as a catalyst for deviant behavior. Psychiatric and alcohol or substance abuse do not explain violent behavior, but this writer agrees with these disturbances and contributes to the understanding of Dark Psychology.

Contemporary social sciences are exploring the areas of psychopathy, narcissism and personality disorders. These profiles are very intriguing and fuel a great deal of interest in the field of forensic and criminal psychology. Based on this author's investigation, there seems to be an intricate combination of these three-character disordered constructs that create truly despotic people. Once this writer has thoroughly presented Dark Psychology, alternative explanations for violent behavior will be provided. Another element of Dark Psychology described will include rapists, pedophiles and sadistic sex offenders.

This writer or researcher will move into the most important themes defining Dark Psychology in the final manuscripts to follow. It is within these areas that the writer offers advice on how to isolate oneself from becoming a future target for human predators. Once you understand Dark Psychology, you will have the ability to assess other people's actions as potentially dangerous.

Employed in mental health for the last two decades, working as a psychologist and forensic examiner for ten years in the treatment of patients, evaluating court-involved defendants, and learning as much as possible as a forensic psychologist, this writer has given the opportunity to offer a set of protective tools to those not involved in the pursuit of Dark Psychology.

Remember, Dark Psychology consists of all criminal and deviant behaviors committed against other people. Although many individuals are intrigued by the discussion of serial killers and psychoanalysts, the vast majority of predators hunting human prey do not engage in murder or sexual deviance. If this writer were to create an estimate, the percentage of human predators would be about 70 percent of the total pool of people who are out to victimize others but are not involved in the murder or sexual deviance. It has been estimated that 30% of offenders include criminal, deviant and violent offenders where physical contact is planned and designed.

In the beginning, this writer or researcher presented what he believes to be a sound theory of the human predator. Dark Psychology assumes that what lives in us all is a potential reservoir of violent malicious energy. All of humanity lies somewhere in the Dark Continuum, most of them in the category of subtle, mild and fleeting thoughts and minor shortfalls. The reality, though, is that Dark Psychology is a universal phenomenon, and there is no dispute that all of us, at times in our lives, have had at least thoughts of pure violence and predatory fantasies.

The difference is that the vast majority of mankind has never acted upon these thoughts. The reason is that we possess a low Dark Factor equation in comparison to predators. For them, their Dark Factor is elevated; it influences them to move in the direction of what many define as evil, and this writer defines it as a trajectory that accelerates toward Dark Singularity.

Carl Jung and Alfred Adler's ideas and theories were a powerful influence in the creation of Dark Psychology by this writer. He strongly connects to Adler's philosophy that behavior is intended. The only slight philosophic divergence from Adler is the writer's belief that all behavior is 99.99 percent objective. He holds the remaining—01 percent as being within the black hole of the Dark Singularity. The black hole in the singularity is the area of evil that the predator has come close to but never reaches.

The Dark Singularity is the potential and zeal in all of us to act as predators to hunt human prey completely and completely without purpose. The writer also strongly endorses Adler's theory of subjective processing. Dark Psychology and human predators have a highly distorted perception filtering mechanism. It is no longer about being caring, compassionate and kind to them—their subjective treatment colors all their considerations, feelings, and perceptions with obscurity and toxic.

At some point in the development of a human predator, he/she is acting on his/her thoughts and feelings, and he/she is going down the long road of what contemporary criminologists call psychophysics. Within time, their subjective filter of processing is divorced from remorse. They come to understand that the victimization of others is well-deserved by those who are too naive to protect themselves.

Given that a huge piece of human development encloses social acknowledgment, the predator some way or another moves into the field where his Dark Factor turns into a functioning power filling a desire to pulverize others. Once the realm of Psychopathy had touched him, he entered the point of no return. Just as light cannot go out of a black hole, the human predator cannot escape the path to the Dark Singularity.

Psychopaths have not only disclosed the perception of experiencing a sense that their evil acts are accelerating in frequency, but also that their experience of acting as predators is of addictive quality. Once again, using cosmology as a metaphor for Dark Psychology, the closer the matter approaches the black hole, the faster the mass accelerates, and the awesome gravity of the black hole can never move away. Psychopathic interviews almost imitate exactly this universal law of astrophysics.

As society moves far away into what is defined as the Information Age of digital technology and cyberspace, Dark Psychology and its impact on humanity will be tested at higher rates. Given the veil of anonymity that cyberspace offers to all humanity, the question remains whether the nefarious aspects of living within all of us will recognize that there is a realm of free reign called the digital universe.

CHAPTER TWO

EMOTIONAL MANIPULATION

If someone is physically or sexually abused, you will most likely be able to see their effects. This is not true when it comes to emotional and mental abuse. The scars are not physical, but they can affect the abused person for the rest of their lives. This is especially true of those who do not seek the help of a professional. Mental manipulation can lead to problems of intimacy, trust, respect and security, just to name a few.

Short-Term Effects

- Surprise and confusion – feeling like what's going on can't possibly be that, wondering why the person who was a friend or loved one is now acting like a complete stranger.

- Self-questioning – you may find yourself wondering if you really remember things right or if something is wrong with you. This is the result of everything you're questioning or telling you to remember things wrongly, and the manipulative party is assumed right.

- Anxiety and vigilance – in order to escape future manipulation, you may become hypervigilant to yourself and others. This is a means of avoiding behavior that might rock a boat or looking for behavior in others that points to an outburst.

- Being passive – as taking action can cause more pain in emotionally abusive relationships, being passive can become a default. It's something that can be hard not to do when you're in a situation that's as stressful as you can be.

- Honest and guilt – you may feel guilty or blame yourself for setting off a manipulative presence in your life. As you may be blamed, it can become harder not to take that out on your own, which makes you feel even worse.

- Avoiding eye contact – you may avoid eye contact and become smaller inside yourself in order to take up less space and feel less likely to be picked up by the manipulator.

- Walking on eggshells – not knowing what causes a spike in the behavior of the other person can lead to over-thinking of every little thing you do to ensure that the manipulator is not upset or angry.

Long-Term Effects of Emotional Manipulation

- Isolation and numbness – you may become an observer rather than a person acting. You may feel little or nothing at all, even in situations that should make you happy. This can make you feel damaged and hopeless, unable to feel emotions again.

- Requiring approval – this manifests itself in ways such as overfulfilling, being kind to everyone, being kind to people, and focusing on appearance. After feeling like you haven't been enough for a long time, your instinct is to make yourself look perfect so that others will appreciate you.

- Feeling resentful – this can be seen as frustration, impatience, irritability, and blame. Resentment will inevitably require release, but it can be difficult to seek and allow. It can be difficult to see anything but that bad behavior after someone treats you badly.

- Excessive judgment – you may find yourself watching for what others are doing and holding people, including yourself, to very high standards. This is a way to feel in control after not being in control. It often takes time and self-compassion to move past.

- Depressive disorder and anxiety – after manipulation or other psychological mistreatment, so many lies have been told that you can often believe them yourself. The good news, in any case, is that it can be healed after some time.

- In addition to these symptoms, Stockholm Syndrome is also common in these types of situations. The person who is abused by the abuser will become accustomed to the abuse and will even defend their painful actions.

Understanding the Tactics and the Manipulative Systems

There are ways in which an emotional manipulator is going to seek power by treating another party poorly. Some of these are common and may be familiar to you if you've ever been in a situation like this. Common tactics include withholding information, gas-lighting, accusing the victim of being confused, shaming, minimizing other people's feelings, and lying. More detailed explanations of common signs are provided below:

Shirking Responsibility

A person who seeks to manipulate you will often avoid taking responsibility for their actions. Instead of taking ownership of the situation and the actions, the manipulator is going to try to twist the situation in such a way that something you did actually lead to the problem.

Denying Past Promises

A person who manipulates you may promise to do anything or offer an affirmative action when asked for something, but they will never do what they said they would do. But if you bring this up, it's going to be turned back on you. They're going to swear you didn't understand what they were saying, and they're going to be forgetful or ridiculous. This can lead you to question yourself and your own memories.

Guilt Tripping

The manipulator is the king or queen of the victim. They may choose to use passive aggression instead of engaging indirectly in aggressive behavior. An example of this might be, "It's fine if you go out with your friends. All I'm going to do is stay here at home alone and clean up the environment.

Ignore Your Problems

Instead of empathizing with you, a manipulator may utilize an opportunity to discuss their own issues.

For example, if you complain about fighting with a family member, it might turn into a diatribe about how at least you have a family to fight with, or how much more often their own fights with family members happen, so you should be thankful.

Not Using Their Words

Instead of talking to you about something that bothers them, a manipulator can talk behind your back or use other passive-aggressive solutions. They may give you the silent treatment, bet, or otherwise show their disapproval without speaking about it. They may choose to say something supportive while showing that the aid is not actually there through their actions.

The Dark Cloud

Manipulators also like to be the center of attention, and they can stop at nothing to do so. If they're upset, they want to make sure everyone knows it. They might do something to show this just to push people to try to make them feel great. It can lead to a very draining and oppressive atmosphere in which to try to deal, especially if this happens frequently.

Wrath and aggression

Intimidation is something on which many manipulative people rely. This can be in the form of anger, veiled threats, or aggressive actions and language. This is even more true when a manipulative party knows that the other person does not like confrontation. By causing you fear and discomfort, you can do whatever you need to make the situation more comfortable, which usually means doing what you wanted.

Looking for the Trust

Manipulators often seek out people who are unsafe, sensitive or trusting. They know that these people are more vulnerable to manipulation and less likely to stop it. By being kind and thoughtful, but calmly and slowly becoming more manipulative, they can begin to exploit a person who is probably already attached to them and wants to avoid waves.

Why Manipulate People

There are many reasons people choose to manipulate others, and they can vary from person to person. Most people sometimes engage in manipulation, but those who primarily interact with manipulation often share certain traits.

- Feelings of helplessness, despair, or worthlessness.
- Fear of abandonment.
- The need for power and control of others.

- Willing to put their feelings on the well-being of others.

- Need to increase self-esteem.

What to Do with A Manipulator

Many people are aware that they are being manipulated, but they are not sure how to handle the problem. The first step to keep in mind is to consider your safety above all else. There are, however, some suggested ways to better understand the other person and their motivations that can be tried.

- Be direct and honest with you. Don't take part in situations that escalate manipulation when you can help.

- Ask questions about the manipulative person and find out if they're going to tell you directly what they want.

- Don't share how manipulative acts make you feel; those feelings are likely to be exploited later.

- Try to avoid being guilty or ashamed of doing something.

- If the other person is threatening you, ask them about this rather than avoiding the problem.

Common Characteristics of Victims

While a skilled manipulator may use emotional manipulation on almost anyone, there are some common themes that manipulators are looking for.

Those who bind their self-worth to meet the needs of others are a common type of victim. Manipulators are attracted to this type of person as they are easy to manipulate, blame, and victimize. By having to meet the needs of others to feel love, this type of person can all the more easily surrender to this sort of abuse.

Individuals who have a difficult time saying no to others are also a common type of manipulator to prey on. If you avoid conflict, it allows the manipulator to do what they want without worrying about any consequences.

People who have trouble showing negative emotions will usually avoid confrontation and keep things happy no matter what. As such, manipulators sometimes seek out these people, as threats may be all they need to do to get whatever they want.

Those who have a poor and weak sense of self often find it difficult to distinguish themselves from the abuser. This makes it particularly difficult to trust your own feelings or to make decisions that will make you happy. Manipulators appreciate that they don't need to try as hard to get what they're after.

Mind Control and Mind Games

Brainwashing (also known as mind control, menticide, persuasion, coercive, thought control, thought reform, and re-education) is the concept that human minds can be altered or controlled by certain psychological techniques. Brainwashing is said to reduce the ability of its subjects to think critically or independently, to allow new, unwanted thoughts and ideas to be introduced into their minds, and to change their attitudes, values and beliefs.

The term "brainwashing" was used in the English language by Edward Hunter in 1950 to describe how the Chinese government seemed to make people coordinate with them. Research into the concept and process also looked at Nazi Germany, some criminal cases in the United States, and the actions of human traffickers. In the 1970s, there was a considerable legal and scientific debate about the brainwashing being a factor in the transformation of youngsters to some new religious movements, often referred to as cults at the time. The concept of brainwashing is sometimes involved in legal proceedings, particularly in relation to child custody. It may also be a theme in science fiction and in political and corporate culture, but it is not generally accepted as a scientific term.

We are aware of a small fraction of the thinking that is going on in our minds, and we can control only a small part of our conscious thoughts. The vast majority of our thinking goes on subconsciously. Only one of these thoughts is likely to break into consciousness at a time. Slips of the tongue and accidental actions give a glimpse of our unfiltered, subconscious mental life.

The meddlesome musings that you may insight for the duration of the day or before bed outline the perplexing actuality that a significant number of the elements of the psyche are outside cognizant ability to control. The central debate on free will is whether we retain true control over any mental function. Perhaps this lack of autonomy is expected as the foundation for almost all the labors of the mind have been laid long before the consciousness of our ancestors evolved.

Even deliberate decisions are not entirely under our power. Our awareness only sets the beginning and the end of the goal but leaves the implementation of unconscious mental processes. As a result, a batter can decide to swing at a ball that enters the strike zone and can delineate the boundaries of that zone. But when the ball comes through, unconscious mental functions take over. The actions required to send him to the first base are too complex and too fast to handle our relatively slow, conscious control.

We exercise some power over our thoughts by directing our attention, like a spotlight, to concentrate on something specific. The consequences of doing so may be amusing, as in the famous experiments in which about one-third of the people watching a basketball game were unable to spot a man in a gorilla suit across the court. Or the consequences can be disastrous as if a narrow focus prevents a driver from seeing a red light or an oncoming train.

Though thoughts appear to "pop" into awareness before bedtime, their cognitive precursors have probably been simmering for a while. Once these preconscious thoughts gather enough strength, the full spotlight of the consciousness beams down upon them. The mind's freewheeling friskiness is only partially under our control, so it's not possible to shut our minds before we sleep.

CHAPTER THREE

BODY LANGUAGE

While the key to success in personal and professional relationships lies in your ability to communicate well, it is not the words you use but your non-verbal cues or "body language" that speak the loudest. Body language is the use of expressions non-verbally, often instinctively rather than consciously.

Whether you know of it or not, when you interact with others, you are constantly giving and receiving wordless signals. All your non-verbal behaviors — the gestures you make, your posture, your tone of voice, how many eyes contact you make — send strong messages. They can ease people, build trust, and bring others to you, or they can offend, confuse, and undermine what you're trying to convey. These messages don't stop when you stop talking. Even when you're silent, you still communicate non-verbally.

In some instances, what you speak and what you communicate through your body language can be two completely different things. If you say a thing, but your body language says something else, your listener is likely to feel you're dishonest. If, for example, you say "yes "while shaking your head, no. When faced with mixed signals like this, the listener must choose whether to believe your verbal or non-verbal message. Since body language is simply a natural and unconscious language that conveys your true feelings and intentions, they are likely to choose a non-verbal message.

However, by building how you understand and use non-verbal communication, you can express what you really mean, better connect with others, and build stronger, more rewarding relationships.

Why Is Non-Verbal Communication Important?

Your non-verbal communication cues — the way you listen, look, move, and react — tell the person you communicate with whether or not you care, whether or not you are true, and how well you listen. When your non-verbal signals match the words you're saying, they increase trust, clarity, and relationship. They can generate tension, mistrust, and confusion when they don't.

If you want to understand how to be a good communicator, you must become more sensitive not only to the body language and non-verbal cues of others but also to your own.

Non-verbal communication can play five roles:

- Repeat: it repeats and often reinforces the message you are making verbally.

- Contradiction: This may contradict the message you are trying to convey, indicating to your listener that you may not be telling the truth.

- Substitution: maybe a substitute for a verbal message. Your facial expression, for example, often conveys a much more vivid message than words can ever convey.

- Complementing: it may add or add to your verbal message. As a boss, if you pat a worker on the back, in addition to giving praise, you can increase your message.

- Accent: it may accentuate or underscore a verbal message. Pounding the table, for example, may underscore the importance of your message.

Types of Non-Verbal Communication

Many different kinds of non-verbal communication or body language include:

Expressions of the face. The human face is extremely expressive, capable of conveying countless emotions without saying a word. And unlike some types and forms of non-verbal communication, facial expressions are universal. Facial expressions of happiness, sadness, anger, surprise, fear, and disgust are the same across cultures.

Movement of the body and posture. Consider how your perceptions of people are assessed by the way they sit, walk, stand or hold their heads. The way you move and carry, you communicate a wealth of information to the world. This kind of non-verbal communication includes your posture, bearing, posture, and the subtle movements you use.

Gestures. Gestures are woven into the pattern of our everyday lives. You may point, wave, beckon, or use your hands to argue or to speak animatedly, often to express yourself with unthinking gestures. However, the meaning of some gestures may be very different across cultures. While the OK sign made by hand, for example, conveys a positive message in English-speaking countries, it is considered offensive in countries such as Germany, Russia and Brazil. So, it's essential to be careful and cautious about how you use gestures to avoid misinterpretation.

Contact with the eye. Since visual sense is dominant for most people, eye contact is a particularly important type of non-verbal communication. The way you look at a person can communicate a lot of things, including interest, affection, hostility, or attraction. Eye contact is also important for maintaining the flow of conversation and for assessing the interest and response of the other person.

Touch it. We communicate a lot through touch. Think about the very different messages given, for example, by a weak handshake, a warm bear hug, a patronizing pat on the head, and a controlling grip on the arm.

Space. Have you ever felt unrelaxed during a conversation because the other person was standing too close to you to invade your space? We all need physical space, although that need varies depending on the culture, the condition and the closeness of the relationship. You can use physical presence to communicate many different non-verbal messages, including signs of intimacy and affection, aggression or dominance.

Voice. It's not just what you're saying, it's what you're saying. When you speak, other people, besides listening to your words, "read" your voice. Things they pay attention to consist of your timing and pace, how loud you are, your tone and sounds that convey understanding. Think about how the tone of your voice can indicate anger, sarcasm, affection, or trust.

Simply put, body language is the undisclosed element of communication that we use to reveal our true feelings and emotions, for example, our gestures, our facial expressions and our posture.

If we can "read" these signs, we can use them to our advantage. For example, it can help us understand the full message of what someone is trying to say to us and increase our awareness of people's reactions to what we say and do.

Body Language and How it Works with Manipulation

We can use it to adjust our body language to make us look more positive, engaging and approachable.

Read the Negative Body Language

Being aware of poor body language in others may allow you to pick up on unspoken issues or bad feelings. So, in this section, we're going to highlight some negative non-verbal signals that you should be looking for.

Difficult conversations and defensiveness

Difficult or tense conversations are an unpleasant fact of life at work. You may have had to handle a difficult customer, or you may have needed to talk to someone about his or her poor performance. Or you might have negotiated a major contract.

Ideally, these situations would have been resolved calmly. But they are often complicated by feelings of nervousness, stress, defensiveness, or even anger. And although we may try to hide them, these emotions are often expressed in the language of our body.

For example, if someone shows one or more of the following behaviors, they are likely to be disengaged, disinterested or unhappy. Be aware of these signs; it can help you adjust what you say and how you say it so that you can make him feel more at ease and more receptive to your point of view.

Avoiding Unengaged Hearings

If you are needed to deliver a presentation or work together in a group, you want the people around you to be 100% engaged.

When you notice someone being disengaged, you're in a better position to do something about it. For instance, you can re-engage her by asking her a direct question or by inviting her to contribute her own ideas.

How to Project Body Language Positively

If you use positive body language, it can add strength to the verbal messages or ideas you want to convey.

Making a First Impression Confident

These tips can help you adjust your body language to make a great first impression:

- Have your posture open. Be relaxed, but please don't slouch! Sit down or stand up and place your hands on your sides. Avoid standing with your hands on your waist, as this will make you appear larger, able to communicate aggression or a desire to dominate.

- Use your firm handshake. But don't get carried away with it! You don't want to make the other person uncomfortable or, worse, painful. If it does, you're likely to come across as rude or aggressive.

- Maintain good contact with the eye. Try to hold the other individual's gaze for a couple of seconds at a time. This is going to show her that you are sincere and engaged. But, do not turn it into a staring match!

- Don't touch your face. There is a common perception that people who touch their faces while answering questions are being dishonest. It's best to avoid fiddling with your hair or touching your mouth or nose, if your goal is to come across as trustworthy.

Public Speech

Positive body language can also help you engage people, mask nerves, and project trust when you speak in public. Here are a few strategies and tips that can help you do this:

- Have a positive attitude. Sit down or stand upright, with your shoulders on your back and your arms unfolded, on your side or in front of you. Don't be tempted to keep your hands in your pockets or slouch, as this will make you look disinterested.

- Keep your head up, please. Your head is supposed to be upright and level. Leaning too far forward or backward may make you look aggressive or arrogant.

- Practice and improve your posture. You would have practiced your presentation beforehand, so why don't you also practice your body language? Stand in a relaxed way, evenly distributing your weight. Keep a foot slightly in front of the other because this will help you maintain your posture.

- Use open hand gestures. Spread your hands apart from each other, in front of you, your palms facing your audience slightly. This indicates a willingness to communicate and share ideas. Keep your upper arms closer to your body. Take care to avoid overexpression, or people might pay more attention to your hands than to what you say.

Interviews, negotiations and reflections

Body language can also help you stay calm in situations where emotions have the potential to run high – a negotiation, for instance, or a performance review. Use the following tips and tactics to defuse tension and to demonstrate openness:

- Use a mirror. If you can, subtly reflect the body language of the person you're talking to, This will make him feel more at ease, and he can build a relationship. But don't copy every gesture he makes, as it may make him feel uncomfortable, or you won't take him seriously.

- Relax the body. It may be hard to keep emotions at bay, especially in nervous situations such as an interview or assessment. But you can keep the appearance of calm by keeping your hands still and avoiding fidgeting with your hair or touching your face.

- Look interested in it. As we suggested above, touching your face or mouth can be a sign of dishonesty. But it can also prove that you're thinking. So, if you're asked a complex question, it's OK to touch your cheek briefly or to stroke your chin. This will show the other individual that you are reflecting on your answer before you respond.

Learn how to manage stress at the moment

Stress is compromising your ability to communicate. When you're stressed out or depressed, you're more likely to misread other people, send out confusing or non-verbal signals, and lapse into unsafe knee-jerk behavior patterns. And remember, the emotions are contagious. If you're upset, it's very likely to make others angry, making a bad situation worse.

If you feel overwhelmed by stress, take your time out. Take a moment to relax before you jump back to the conversation. You will feel better equipped to deal with the situation in a positive way.

The quickest and safest way to calm down and manage the stress of the moment is to use your senses — what you see, hear, smell, taste, and touch — or a soothing movement. By review a photograph of your child, smelling a most loved aroma, tuning in to a bit of music, or crushing a pressure ball, for instance, you can rapidly unwind and re-center. Since everybody reacts in an unexpected way, you may need to examination to locate the sensory experience that turns out best for you.

Develop an emotional awareness

You can have full control of your emotions and how they influence you in order to send accurate non-verbal cues. You also need to be able to identify the emotions of others and the true feelings behind the cues they're sending out. This is where emotional awareness is coming in.

Being emotionally aware allows you to:

- Read other people exactly, including the emotions they feel and the unspeakable messages they send.

- Create trust in relationships by sending non-verbal signals that match your words.

- Respond in ways that indicate that you understand and care about yourself.

Many of us are disconnected from our emotions — especially strong emotions such as anger, sadness, fear — because we have been taught to try to shut down our feelings. But as long as you can deny or numb your feelings, you can't eliminate them. They're still there, and they still affect your behavior. However, by developing your emotional awareness and connecting with unpleasant emotions, you will gain greater control over how you think and act.

How to read your Body Language

Once you've built up your capacities to oversee pressure and perceive feelings, you'll begin to improve by perusing the non-verbal signs sent by others. It's important to:

Pay attention to inconsistencies, please. Non-verbal communication should reinforce what has been said. Is the person saying one thing, but the body language conveys something else? For example, don't they say "yes "to you while shaking their head?

Look at non-verbal communication signals as a group. Don't read too much in a single gesture or a non-verbal note. Consider all the non-verbal signals you receive, from eye contact to voice and body language. Taken together, are their non-verbal cues consistent — or inconsistent — with what their words say?

Trust your instincts, please. Don't let go of your gut feelings. If you feel that someone isn't honest or that something doesn't add up, you might pick up on the mismatch between verbal and non-verbal cues.

Evaluating non-verbal signals

Eye contact – Is the person making contact with the eye? If so, is that too intense or just right?

Facial expression – What does their face show? Is it masked and non-expressive, or is it emotionally present and filled with interest?

The tone of voice – Does the person's voice project warmth, trust, and interest, or is it strained or blocked?

Posture and gesture – Is the body relaxed, stiff and immobile? Are their shoulders tense, raised, or relaxed?

Touch – Is there any kind of physical contact? Is that appropriate for the situation? Does that make you feel uncomfortable?

Intensity – Does the person seem flat, disinterested, cool or over-the-top and exaggerated?

Timing and Place – Is there any easy flow of information back and forth? Do non-verbal responses come too quickly or too slowly?

Sounds – Do you hear sounds that indicate a person's interest, care or concern?

CHAPTER FOUR

STAGES IN DEVELOPMENT OF THE MANIPULATION

Under this model, the phases of manipulation and coercion leading to exploitation are explained as follows:

Targeting stage. The suspected abuser or offender may:

- Look for young individuals who may already be vulnerable, such as young people who are sad, lonely, sexually reactive or who are using alcohol or any other drugs;

- Try to comprehend the youngster and distinguish their interest;

- Become friends with a young person, show care for them, give gifts or compliments;

- Achieve the trust of the young person

- Share the information of the young person with other abusive adults.

The Friendship-The Forming Stage. The suspected abuser or offender may:

- Make a great deal of effort to become someone that the young person can trust and rely on.

- To make the young person feel special.

- to be qualified to understand the young person in a way other people do not;

- Give them goodies, gifts and rewards;

- Listen to and value the young people;

- Ask the young individual to keep secrets about what they do together.

- Support young people and be their 'best friend.'

- Test physical contact by "accidentally" touching them

- Offer protection to young people against harassment by peers or abusive adults.

Love the relationship stage. Once trust has been established, the alleged abuser or offender may:

- Become a young man's 'boyfriend' or 'girlfriend.'

- Isolate young people from their friends and family in such a way that they feel dependent on them (and their network) for friendship and social ties;

- Establish a sexual relationship;

- Reduce the inhibitions of young people, for example, by showing them pornography

- engage young people in illegal activities, such as drinking alcohol or taking drugs

- To be inconsistent in their affection, for example, to make promises that they will not keep or be loving one day and distant the next day.

- Ask the young individual to keep secrets about what they do together

- Support the young person

- Offer protection to young people against harassment by peers or abusive adults.

Abuse the relationship stage. The suspected abuser or offender may:

- Remove friendship and love

- Ask for sex

- Trafficking in young people for sex

- Strengthen dependence by lowering young people's self-esteem, verbally abusing or degrading them;

- Isolate young people from friends and family

- Trick the young person to stay in the relationship by saying they owe them money or make other threats.

How to Identify Manipulators and Manipulators Predators

Assemble data to distinguish the beginning phases of control and compulsion before the youngster is trapped in a pattern of sexual exploitation.

The modern methodologies utilized by guilty parties to control, pressure and quietness youngsters may make it hard to distinguish beginning phases of manipulation and coercion where abusive dynamics have not yet taken hold. This table helps practitioners work sensitively with the young person to understand their relationship and identify sexual exploitation before they become trapped.

Identification of manipulative behavior

Manipulation is an emotionally unhealthful psychological strategy used by people who are incapable of asking what they want and need directly, "says Sharie Stines, a California-based therapist who specializes in abuse and toxic relationships.

There are many different ways of manipulation, ranging from a busy salesman to an emotionally abusive partner — and some behaviors are easier to spot than others.

Feeling fear, obligation, and guilt.

Manipulative behavior, according to Stines, involves three factors: fear, obligation and guilt. "When someone is manipulating you, you're psychologically forced to do something that you probably don't want to do," she says. You might feel scared to do it, forced to do it, or guilty of not doing it.

She points to two common manipulators: "the sniper" and "the victim." A sniper makes you feel fearful and might use aggression, threats and intimidation to control you, she says. The victim generates a sense of guilt in the target. "The victim is usually hurt," says Stine. But while the manipulators often play the victim, the reality is that they are the ones who caused the problem, she adds.

A person targeted by the manipulators who play the victim often tries to help the manipulator stop feeling guilty, Stines says. Targets of this type of manipulation often feel responsible for helping the victim do whatever they can to stop their suffering.

You question yourself

The term "gaslighting" is used to identify manipulations that get people to question themselves, their memory, reality, or thoughts. A manipulative individual may contort what you say, commandeer a discussion, or cause you to feel as you've accomplished something incorrectly when you're not exactly sure you've done it.

If you're gas-fired, you might feel a false sense of guilt or defense — like you've completely failed, or you must have done something wrong when, in reality, that's not the case, according to Stines.

"The manipulators are to blame," she says. "They're not taking responsibility."

There are strings attached to it.

If you don't get a favor just because of it, it's not for fun and free. "If the strings are attached, then the manipulation is done."

Stines refers to a type of manipulator as' Mr. Nice Guy.' This person may be helpful and do a lot of favors to other people. "It's very confusing because you don't realize there's anything negative going on," she says. "But, on the other hand, with good deeds, there is a string attached — an expectation." If you do not meet the manipulator's expectations, you will be made to be ungrateful, Stines says.

The exploitation of the norms and expectations of reciprocity is one of the most common forms of manipulation, says Jay Olson, a Ph.D. researcher studying manipulation at McGill University.

For example, a salesperson might make it look like you should buy the product because he or she gave you a deal. In a relationship, a partner may buy you flowers and then ask for something in return. "These tactics are working because they abuse social norms," says Olson. "It's normal to reciprocate favors, but even if someone does one insincerely, we often still feel compelled to reciprocate and comply."

You see the 'foot-in-the-door' and 'door-in-the-face' techniques.

Manipulators often try one of two tactics, says Olson. The first is a foot-in-the-door technique that starts with a small and reasonable request — like, do you have the time? — which leads to a larger request — like I need $10 for a taxi. "This is commonly used in street scams," says Olson.

The door-in-the-face technique is the opposite — it involves someone making a big request, rejecting it, then making a smaller one, Olson explains.

For example, someone doing contract work may ask you for a large amount of money upfront, and then, after you decline, ask for a smaller amount, he says. This works because, compared to the larger application, the smaller appeal appears reasonable, says Olson.

What to do if you are manipulated

How you react to manipulation depends to a large extent on what kind of manipulation you're facing.

A good support group, too, says Stines. "Individuals in toxic relationships need to hear counterpoints. They're conditioned to think the interactions are normal. Somebody needs to help them get out of that assumption.

For other kinds of manipulation, Stines suggests trying not to allow manipulative behavior to assess you personally. "Use the motto, 'Observe but don't absorb,'" she says. After all, "We're not responsible for the feelings of anyone else."

Defining borders can often play an important role in keeping manipulation at bay. "People who manipulate have lousy borders," says Stines. "You have your own voluntary experience as a human being, and you need to know where you end up and where the other person begins. Manipulators often have either too rigid or enmeshed boundaries.

It can help to delay your response in a manipulative situation, according to Olson. For example, refrain from signing a contract at first glance, do not make a large purchase without thinking about it, and avoid making major relationship decisions for the first time, he suggests. "Sleeping on it" is often the best way to avoid being manipulated, "Olson adds.

CHAPTER FIVE

EMOTIONAL MANIPULATION IN A RELATIONSHIP

Manipulation is very common in relationships today than ever before. With the increase in social media and the decrease in interpersonal skills, people have become more and more manipulative.

But the manipulation of relationships is not always the result of evil intent. It's innocent and harmless a lot of times. In most cases, the person making the manipulation is not even aware that they are manipulating their partner. They are aware of it in some cases, but they believe it is harmless. Manipulation is part of a toxic relationship, and it's going on forever.

But you're supposed to be wary of any kind of manipulation in the relationship. Even though it may be harmless, manipulation can soon turn into a toxic pattern if you don't handle it properly and talk to your partner about it.

Let's look at a couple of common types of manipulation in a relationship:

1. Cover Contracts

The term "Cover Contract" is described by Dr. Robert Glover in his book "No More Mr. Nice Guy." This form of manipulation is very common in men who are insecurity in a relationship. But it can be seen in women as well.

A covert contract is a contract that many people make in their minds, but they never really discuss it with their partner. They're going to do something nice for their partner and expect something in return.

For example, "I'm going to buy her the dress she liked. I'm sure she's going to have sex with me tonight.

Or the extreme case of such a contract might be something like, "I'll pay for her education and support her in her career. In return, I'm sure she's going to love me and stay loyal to me.

Of course, when it doesn't go as planned, they're going to get angry, and it's going to lead to a fight. Sometimes they hold their anger inside, and it festers until it blows up. But such manipulation does not lead to anything good.

2. The Trap

"Do you think that in that dress she looks good? "Yeah, sure of that. "I knew that you liked her. How long have you been obsessive about her? A common form of manipulation that people use is a trap for their partner.

It might be as simple as a word trap. Or something extremely complicated and manipulative, like getting a friend to hit their partner. In either case, it is wrong to do this and how you should react depends on their intentions and the reasons behind the manipulation.

3. The Silent Treatment

The Still Treatment Silent treatment is the preferred type of manipulation for many people.

Instead of talking about the issue at hand, they choose to give their partner a silent treatment. Now, the silent treatment is not bad in itself.

Often, being silent and thinking about the matter can help you conclude. But some people do that to punish their partner and win the argument. But if they keep silent until you say you're sorry, even if you weren't wrong, then you have a master manipulator at your fingertips, and you need to get to grips with this issue as soon as possible.

4. Checking Your Messages

Check Your Messages Another type of manipulation people use is to constantly check your messages behind your back or in front of you.

It is a disregard of trust and an invasion of privacy in most cases.

But some people understand how to manipulate their partners to accept this behavior. They're going to say things like, "If you don't have anything to hide, why do you care? This type of manipulation is common in relationships where one partner has trust issues. These trust issues are often the result of something that has happened in the relationship.

But in many cases, these trust issues are simply one partner's uncertainty about the relationship.

5. Social Media

Social media have made manipulation very easy. You will often find passive-aggressive comments and a shipload of different manipulative tactics used by people who love social media manipulation.

If your partner uses social media to manipulate you, it's most likely that they're doing it to make you jealous or to put you down. They can do things like that,

- Post photos with someone of the opposite sex.
- Post-passive-aggressive quotations that may be directed at you. Things like, "If you can't take care of me at my worst, you don't deserve me at your best."
- Actively like and comment on the status or pictures of an ex or a person they know you are jealous of.

6. Withholding sex to get what they want

The thing that comes first in their mind is a very direct manipulation that many people see in their relationship. It's quite common with women, but it's also known for men to do this.

They withhold sex from the partner because they don't get what they want. They sometimes withhold sex to punish a partner for doing something they didn't like.

"Don't you take out the trash? Well, don't expect anything to happen tonight.

"Didn't you buy me the necklace that I wanted? You're not going to see me naked until you do that.

Retaining sex is not always a big deal in a healthy relationship. So, if your partner is just trying to tease you or they're playing, it's all right, and you shouldn't worry about it.

It's also understandable if they're upset about something with you, and they need time to let go of their anger before they can feel comfortable enough to have sex. But it's going to be an issue when they stop sex just to punish you or get something out of you.

To find out if this is manipulation or if your partner is upset with you, you need to wear a little empathic hat and try to see how you're going to react if you're in their situation.

Have you lied to them about something big and feel they can't trust you right now?

Understandably, they don't want to have sex right now because they don't trust you.

Give them a little time and listen to them.

Try to talk about this and come to a solution together. Treat them with regard, respect and understanding, and they will soon begin to trust you again. Are they angry because you didn't get them the birthday gift they wanted? If so, there's a better chance that they just want you to get the money, and they're trying to "train" you to do what they want.

7. The Controller of Life

This type of manipulation is very subtle. Because you're not even going to realize they're manipulating you.

It'll feel like they're helping you out. But in reality, they're going to control your life and shape it the way they want it. Now let me be clear and precise; healthy couples support each other and help each other make important life decisions.

If you have a partner who has control of all parts of your life, you will eventually stop feeling like yourself and feel like you're living someone else's life. It's a good initiative and idea to confront them and talk about it before resenting them and ending up in a bad breakup.

Addressing the manipulation of the relationship Handling manipulation in a relationship comes down to three things:

1. Introspection

The first step, introspection, is to look into yourself and ask yourself if you have done something to justify this manipulation. Did your partner try to talk to you, and did you ignore them?

Have you neglected some of the needs that your partner has told you about?

Most importantly, have you been doing some kind of manipulation that has caused your partner to manipulate in return?

It is important to be honest with yourself.

If you're unsure, it will help you talk to someone close to you and get their opinion on the subject.

If you choose to talk about it with someone else, make sure you give them an unbiased view of what happened.

2. Intent and Show Empathy

The second step is to determine your partner's intention. In other words, it's about putting yourself in their shoes and trying to feel what they were feeling.

Your goal here is to try to understand them and figure out where they're coming from.

Is your partner manipulative because they're unsafe and don't know how to communicate properly? Or is it that they're just upset about something serious, and this manipulation is just a way to get some kind of validation from you?

If you're not sure about their intentions, it's best not to make any assumptions about them. Instead, just talk to them about it.

When you talk to them, make sure that you understand them and conclude, not to blame them and get the moral higher ground.

3. Communications

The third step and key, communication, is the most important.

With proper communication, you can solve a lot of problems in your relationship. You may not be able to solve your partner's childhood problems and bad habits that have arisen over the years. But you can bring these problems to light and find a way to tackle them together.

Remember, whenever you choose to communicate, do so clearly and to resolve the issue. " I want to make your relationship work, and I want us to communicate better. I want to understand why you did that. Is that because [your idea of their intention]? If your partner gets angry and annoyed, remind them that you love them.

You just want to understand them and make sure you can communicate with each other. If they don't want to work on the issues and discuss them, even after trying multiple times, then there's a good chance that your partner isn't willing to learn and grow.

And you're supposed to seriously consider ending that relationship. In the relationship, manipulation can turn into a toxic behavioral pattern.

It's best to deal with manipulation as soon as possible. The more you ignore it, the more difficult it will be to recognize the behavior and change it. It will take some effort on both partners to get rid of toxic manipulation in your relationship.

If one partner is unwilling to make an effort, it's best to consider ending the relationship. Sign You are Manipulated

1. The Old Plain Bullying This is one of the less subtle (and more easily recognizable) forms of manipulation.

For example, your partner is asking you if you want to clean up their cars. You're not. You're trying to say no. But the look on their faces and the tone in their voice says that you're better off cleaning their car or that something bad is going to go down. So, you say, "I'd love to do it!" and then you do it. This is an individual who utilizes the danger of savagery to control you and get you to consent to accomplish something you would prefer not to do. Later, they might say things like, "You didn't have to do that; you might have said no." This makes it look like a good guy like it's your fault that you didn't get your job done because you were too bust out of their car. Sneaky, mean. This is a tough answer because it's safer to do what the manipulator wants at that time and then figure out how to escape later.

Some of the abusers will use real violence to get what they want. But in some cases, you can start to say "no" and mean "no." If you can't say the word "no" in a relationship without fearing for your safety, you need to get out of there.

2. Advantage of the Home Court Manipulation is all about control.

One of the tactics and tips used to gain control is to get a person out of their element. Think about where you live, where you hang out, whose friends you're visiting, and where you're going on dates. Are all the favorite spots of your partner? Do you live in the life of your partner, but they don't live in yours? This could be a manipulation strategy designed to make your partner feel in control. You're easier to control when you're not relaxed in the surroundings. What to do: the equal advantage of the home court.

It's 50-50. You both live in the lives of each other. Both of you have chosen places to go to dates. You both just go to places where you feel comfortable. It's part of a healthy, equal relationship.

3. Tugging your heartstrings Let's say that your partner is going to find a kitten.

The non-manipulative approach would be to know how you feel about getting a kitten, discuss whether you could afford vet care and food, find out how your landlord feels about kittens, and determine if it was the best choice for both you and the kitten. The manipulative approach aims to tugging your heartstrings and making you feel like a bad person if you say no. It's like, "Look at his little face! He's homeless! Do you want him to die and alone in the streets? Do you even have a heart?" There's a big difference. Don't let a person make you feel like making the best choice to make you a bad person.

You don't have to carry the kitten home in this situation to ensure it's survival. You can find another home or take it to a shelter for adoption. Most of these types of manipulations are subject to reasonable alternatives.

4. If you loved me, This is the worst thing.

This manipulation asks you to prove your love repeatedly by giving your partner what they want. "If you loved me, you'd go to the store and get me some ice cream!" or even, "If you loved me, you'd change your intentions about having a baby." This one uses emotion and guilt to try and shame you into doing something. It's a kind of manipulation, no matter how innocent that sounds. What to do, shut it down.

Say something like, "I will still love you with my whole heart without going to the store to get you some ice cream." You can also ask for direct communication. Like, "You know that you can just ask me to go to the store. You don't have to put my love for you on it.

5. The Blackmail Emotional

Emotional blackmail is bad, and there are not many ways to lead to a healthy relationship. It looks like, "I'm going to kill myself if you leave." Or, it can also look like, "I'm going to die without you." It can be dramatic or casual. It's a tactic that uses fear, guilt, and shame to keep you under your partner's control.

It's always a manipulation and never a real threat of suicide or self-harm. But in order to be safe, say, "If you feel suicidal, I'll call the police or the ambulance for help, but I'm not going to deal with it." It sounds tough, but it's often the best (and only) thing you can do.

6. Playing with the victim

Let me hurt a scenario for you. You and your partner get into a situation that led to quarrels and fights. No matter who's wrong, what's been said, or what's gone down, your partner is just heartbroken and can't believe you're going to hurt them like that. Even if your partner is the one who did something wrong, and no matter how you reacted. You're always apologizing that your partner is always hurt and helpless and in need.

What to do: You can apologize for what you feel you have to apologize for. Don't give in to your partner's continuous attempts to shame you into falling on your sword. Say things like, "I'm sorry I got upset and raised my voice.

That was not called for. But I'm not apologizing for being upset about what you did. This is how it made me feel. "Prepare for the work of water.

7. Gaslighting

Gaslighting is the form of manipulation that is most likely to make you feel like you're losing your dang mind. Your partner does shade things consistently, as if they pretend not to say things, pretend not to say things, leave out information, twist the truth, reinvent the past, make you think that you've forgotten things, and make you feel like you're losing things in general. When it's done enough, you're going to feel like you can't trust your brain, so you need your partner to keep you in check.

What to do: get out of here. Gaslighting is a serious form of abuse, simple and simple.

8. Convenient Needs

If things don't go your partner's way, are they sick or weak or in need of care and support? This is a form of manipulation, even if your partner is sick. Examples: your partner doesn't need to have a good conversation with you, so they feel faint. Your partner doesn't want to go anywhere, and all of a sudden, you can't go either because they need you to help them with their anxiety (which is conveniently fine once you agree to stay at home). Your partner can't help you with your housework because they have a headache or no energy. Your partner doesn't want you out of their life because who's going to take care of them? Or maybe they're fake illness, so you're going to feel sorry for them and give them some more attention.

What to do: this is not a good relationship, and you probably want to think about leaving. But right now, you can make a plan on how to take care of your partner while you're going to do what you need to do. Odds are, they're going to be fine.

9. Killing them by Kindness.

Kindness as manipulation is particularly damaging because it makes you question people's motives whenever they're nice to you. An easy example of this is the great scenario where someone gives someone else a gift or a string of compliments, and the other person says, "OK, what do you want?" , "You're just so smart, I don't know why you're not going to school," when the real motivation is to have a partner who makes more money and not their happiness.

What to do: Kindness with an ulterior motive is not Kindness. You can say thank you for being kind, but you still can't give in to the controlling aspect of manipulation. If you can see it, remember, no shame if you're not going to catch it. Manipulators are so stupid.

10. They're calm, cool, and they're collected

There's something wrong with women, there's a conflict, or things seem to be in chaos. Is your partner super calm? This could be a manipulation that makes you feel like you're overreacting. It might make you feel like you can't trust your emotional reactions. It's the way your partner controls your emotional reactions. They determine when a situation requires an emotional response. Otherwise, you're just going to be dramatic or stupid. Because it's super calm, they can call your mental health or maturity into question, and over time, you may not even realize that you're looking for them to respond when something happens.

What to do: If you are an individual who often falls for this manipulation,, you may require treatment to assist you with getting back in contact and trust your actual emotion. That is the manner by which harming this sort of control can be. The best thing you can do right presently is to go with your gut and recall that you don't need to legitimize your sentiments to anybody.

11. They're always just kidding

This is a two-part manipulation. The initial segment is where they express harmful things or criticize you, but isn't your fault to get upset because they were just kidding. It doesn't matter how cruel they were; it's just that you're too sensitive, and you can't take a joke. The second part involves making jokes about you both in public and in front of others. If you respond negatively to others, you're going to make a scene, or you're going to ruin the fun. This is a way to dig in and grind you down without having to take responsibility for it.

What to do: you don't need to worry about ruining the fun or being too sensitive. It may be hard to confront your partner when they hurt you and risk looking like a bad guy, but it's important to stand up for yourself even if the manipulator is likely to try to shame you.

The more you perceive manipulative practices, the more you will have the option to close them down. However, if you're dealing with a serious manipulator, ads are your best bet to split.

CHAPTER SIX

HOW TO PERSONALLY USE THE

DARK PERSUASION

Understanding the theories of motivation, persuasion, and influence will put you in the driver's seat of life. Why? Why? Because all you want or want in life comes from these three simple concepts. Did you know that less than 1% of the world's population understands and can apply the twelve laws of persuasion? Therefore, as I say the secrets of influence and the science of persuasion, you will be able to convince and influence with 99 percent accuracy. You'll gain instant influence over others and inspire others to take action, while you'll get what you want from life. You will win individuals to your way of thinking and empower yourself with unshakeable trust. You're going to triple your sales and marketing prosperity. You will be a captivating magnet of success.

As you create what I call Magnetic Persuasion, others will be pulled in to you as metal filings are attracted to an amazing magnet. You will have financial, social and personal success. Gateways that were previously closed to you will swing wide open, and the world of opportunity will beat a path to your door. The life-changing abilities and techniques described in this book are based on timeless, proven principles. They have been developed from countless times of persuasion research and exhaustive studies of human nature. And now, for the first time, you're being unveiled.

This guide teaches the twelve critical Laws of Persuasiveness and teaches you how to use these cutting-edge strategies of persuasion so that you can gain the influence you need NOW. You're going to learn how to make people instinctively like and trust you, something that might otherwise take you years to do. You might no longer face the unexpected with tension, fear or intimidation. Instead, you will face it head-on with credibility, control, and trust. Day in and day out, you'll turn every challenge you face into a winning situation. In short, you are going to be the master of your own destiny.

In today's world, the power of persuasion is of extraordinary and critical importance. Almost every human encounter involves an attempt to gain influence or to convince others of our way of thinking. Irrespective of age, profession, religion or philosophy, people are always trying to convince each other. We all want to be able to convince and influence others to listen, trust, and follow us. An ongoing report by financial analysts found that 26 percent of GDP was legitimately owing to the utilization of influence abilities in the marketplace.1 Persuasion is the driving force of our economy. Consider it—$2.3 trillion of our gross domestic products comes from the power of persuasion and influence. You rarely see large corporations lowering their sales forces. Sales professionals are assets of the company, not liabilities.

Advertisers spend billions of dollars analyzing and researching our psychographics and demographics to find out how to subtly convince us. Rosselli, Skelly, and Mackie point out that "even conservative estimates show that an average person is exposed to 300 to 400 persuasive media messages per day from mass media alone." Every day, we are filled with thousands of persuasive messages through a myriad of sources, including newspapers, magazines, billboards, signs, packaging, the Internet, direct mail, radio, TV, mail orders, catalogs, coworkers. The question is: are these tips and tactics being used for or against you? Thousands, even millions, are persuaded every day against their better judgment, simply because they are unfit to interpret and respond effectively to the publicity barrier that we face forever. In this case, what you don't understand is going to hurt you. Persuasive influences flood our daily lives and are inescapable. It is with no question in our best interest to master Magnetic Persuasion, to know how it works, and to learn how to implement its proven techniques so that we are empowered today.

Persuasion is a process of changing or reforming attitudes, beliefs, opinions or behavior towards a predetermined outcome through voluntary compliance. Persuasion is what you do and say.

Influence-is who you are and how you, as a person, will have an impact on the message. This includes whether you are considered to be trustworthy or your passion.

Power-increases your ability to convince and influence people. This power can be seen with individuals who possess the knowledge, have authority, or use coercion in the process of persuasion.

Motivation is the ability to encourage others to act in accordance with the suggestions and ideas you have put forward. Motivation is your "call for action" or what you want your audience to do.

Let's be honest: we all need and want other people's stuff. We want people to follow us, trust us, and accept us. We want to influence others in our way of thinking. We're trying to get what we want when we want it. Having the right tools and knowing how to use them is a secret to success.

Maximum influence provides a complete toolbox for effective persuasion techniques. Most people use the same limited tools of persuasion over and over, with only temporary, limited, or undesired outcomes.

We need to clear our minds to the entire toolbox of persuasion and influence. We've all heard the maxim, "If the only tool you've got is a hammer, you tend to see every problem as a nail." The problem is, everyone isn't a nail. The art of persuasion must be tailored to every group or individual, every situation or event. It's like playing the keyboard with only two or three notes: you play "Chopsticks" when you're supposed to play Mozart. You can make a masterpiece with your life when you play with all the keys of persuasion and influence.

Persuasion is also your golden promotion ticket. Relational abilities rank number one of the apparent multitude of individual characteristics that businesses look for in school graduates. Master communicators feel in control of circumstances since they comprehend the craft of influence and ability to perceive and use persuasive strategies.

Learning how to convince and influence will make a difference between hoping for a better income and having a better income. Beware of the common mistakes that presenters and persuaders commit to, making them lose the deal.

Persuasion is a missing puzzle piece that cracks the code to dramatically increase your income, improve your relationship, and help you get what you want, when you want, and win your friends for life. Ask yourself how much money and income you've lost because of your inability to convince and influence. Think about that. Sure, you've seen a little success, but think of the times when you couldn't get it done. Have you ever had a time when you didn't get your point across? Were you unable to convince a person to do anything about it? Have you achieved your full potential? What about your relationship, huh? Feel more sure about your capacity to persuade.

Proficient achievement, individual joy, administration potential, and pay rely upon the capacity to persuade, impact, and inspire others.

The power of persuasion can open doors to you and make the path to success much smoother. You will have a range of persuasive techniques at your disposal after reading this article.

The most persuasive tricks and techniques have their roots in NLP (neurolinguistic programming). These techniques of persuasion are based on empathy-to convince someone-you have to understand them.

Empathy-Based Persuasive Technology

The most significant thing you need to understand about the person you're trying to influence is what their mind responds best-feel, visual or auditory stimulation. Realizing this will make it simpler for you to be more persuasive by connecting and taking care of this specific desire.

Women usually respond best to feelings, but not always. Men frequently respond well to visuals, and some people are affected by audio. To learn the best stimulation to focus your persuasion, look at how they're talking. Do they say, "I can see," "I can hear what you say," These are clear examples, the right answer could be more inconspicuous and maybe a combination of two sorts of incitement.

Adjust your persuasion techniques based on the form of mind you're dealing with; for example, when persuading someone who's "feel" oriented, focus on how they feel when they do what you're trying to convince them to do. Don't try and tell them what it's going to be like you've got to make them feel it.

The more you know the person you're dealing with, the more effectively you're going to be able to focus on your persuasive techniques.

Mirror-Based Persuasive Technology

Matching your body language and your posture/position is a subtle but surprisingly powerful persuasive technique. You should be unobtrusive and may feel awkward from the outset, yet with some training, you will perceive how successful this procedure, known as "mirroring," can be in building up a relationship and facilitating persuasion.

People respond better to persuasive techniques in their own "language." Pick up specific words that they use and use back on them, especially adjectives. Pay attention to their pitch, speed and volume, and respond in the same way as possible.

Be Persuasive by Connecting Emotionally, Not Rationally

Anyone in politics is going to tell you-people just don't respond rationally. They respond on the basis of emotions. To convince someone, you need to have an emotional connection with them.

Aristotle identified the three basic elements of each persuasive argument:

Ethos: the credibility, knowledge, expertise, stature and authority of the person trying to convince.

Logos: the appeal of logic, reasoning, cognitive thinking, data and facts.

Pathos: appeal to emotions; non-cognitive, non-thinking motivations that affect decisions and actions.

Of course, all layers are important, but it is perhaps the emotional layer that holds the most power of persuasion. We are emotional beings, and we are much more likely to be persuaded by the promise of feeling good than the promise of "being right."

Is Persuasion Techniques Moral?

Of course, you might think that using persuasion techniques is immoral, underhand. Indeed, you may find yourself faced with the dilemma of whether to use it on someone you love. It's up to you, really, how you feel about using persuasive techniques, but remember the following.

People need to be aware of the techniques and know when others are trying to manipulate them. If you succeed in persuading someone, you simply out-compete them.

Persuasion is always an option. Yet, after a lot of practice, you may find that these persuasive techniques are simply part of the nature of your being. Would you feel guilty about using any other aspects of your personality, such as speaking confidently?

Much of the time, you're going to try to do what's best for them anyway. The purpose of emotionally connecting with someone is to learn what they want. If you know this, you're just persuading them to do something they're going to do anyway. So, by definition, persuasion is not manipulation-it's just bringing your point across.

People should be sufficiently aware of making their own decisions. Ideally, you should be more confident that you can use these persuasive techniques to do what's right for all concerned.

The secret to the universe is the power of persuasion. Persuasion is the key to getting what you want, becoming rich and having success in everything. Nothing can be done without persuasion. It's a matter of persuading yourself and others. Persuasion is about moving consciousness, and if you can move consciousness, you can move anything in the universe. All persuasion persuades us to take action, be it mental or physical. All the rich and successful people are the masters of persuasion.

You may have had some ideas against using persuasion because you think it's manipulation. But those are the limiting beliefs that you have that are stopping you from succeeding. The use of persuasion for wrongful reasons is manipulation, but the natural use of persuasion is for the sake of direction. People want to be controlled in a way that makes them eager and comfortable to take action to benefit themselves. We all naturally want to be led by someone who can show us the way to do what's good for us.

Realize that perception is creating reality. Persuasion is about changing people's perceptions in order to change their reality. It's about helping others see things in a way they haven't seen before. In order to use persuasion, you must first convince yourself of the use of persuasion. You've got to change your perception of persuasion. When you can shift your perception and belief of reality to those who are rich and successful, you can use the power of persuasion in the way they use it.

The most common, powerful and influential people in the world are persuasive. They have the power to shift people's perceptions, beliefs, and ideas about things. If you want to transform the world, you need to change people's consciousness. The most powerful form of persuasion is persuasion that moves people in the direction they want to go. It's persuasion to show them the means to get what they want. You can persuade individuals to do anything if they think it's going to satisfy them.

In all persuasion, the aim is to convince people that they have a certain desire, and can satisfy that desire, and that it is worth what they give in exchange for what they want. There are many areas that teach persuasion in different ways, but the fundamental principles are all down to the few that represent everything. It's all about getting attention and sparking interest and curiosity. Then it's about arousing desire and persuading them to take some action to fulfill that desire.

The key thing all persuasion deals with is to convince others of the value of something. Something has value on the basis of the value you give it. Who can say that a certain amount of money is worth a particular product? The truth is, everything in the universe is free. People's perceptions value all things in life. The perception of value can vary from person to person. You can create any value in anything by simply causing others to perceive it.

Nothing in the realm is of any use to any being except the consciousness that the being has toward it. All drugs and medicines will not work to heal if a person believes that they would not heal and that their conscience is not in harmony for healing, but for the disease. For a person who has a conscience and a belief in healing, even a placebo would have the effect of healing. No one can obtain satisfaction from anything unless they have a conscience to obtain satisfaction from that thing.

It's persuasion that makes the world go round. If people were not persuaded to do anything, there would be no movement of energy. There would be no purchase or sale. When resources are not moved around, things cannot be placed in the hands of those who can make better use of them. The economy comes to a pause when money doesn't flow. If people keep what they have instead of giving to obtain something more, it will only lead to stagnation, entropy, and degrading of the universe.

That's why marketers and sales promoters are really doing a great service to society. By persuading people to see value in something and to give something else, whether it is time, money or resources, to obtain it, they are encouraging the exchange of energy. When energy is exchanged, that is when new combinations and advanced forms of energy can be created for the benefit of the rest of the world. The exchange of energy is what promotes the evolution of humanity and the advancement of life.

Persuasion is the power that can make people buy trash or treasure. If people who use very persuasive and compelling messages to influence people to buy trash, doesn't that give you every reason to use the same kind of powerful persuasion to influence people to buy treasure instead? You can sell them the moon, the stars, and the cosmic system with regards to elevating what you have to bring to the table on the grounds that the worth is made by perception, and you do them a favor by leading them to yours instead.

The forces of the market are influenced by supply and demand. Even supply and demand are based on perception. You never have to worry about supply and demand when you can create demand through persuasion and convince others to see you as their best supply. You can create your own market with the power of persuasion, and that's why it's called marketing. The power to influence is the power to create wealth.

The way to great wealth is to create as much value as possible to others. Since value is created by perception, the value can be created by creating a perception of value. The higher the perception of value that you are able to create and the more people you are able to influence, the more you can create an exchange of energy where money flows to you in exchange for what you offer.

Favorites Victims

Perhaps you would like to think that deep down, everyone has good intentions. Unfortunately, this is probably not the case. A lot of people are willing to use you and walk all over you if it means going to the top. When you're dealing with an experienced manipulator, you often don't realize what happened until it's too late. How often are you being manipulated by others? Are you too confident about that? Or can you see the bad intentions of a person a mile away?

Here are seven signs that you can't easily manipulate:

1. You are asking for respect from others

People who enjoy manipulating others seek low-esteem targets. They know that it's easier to get what they want from someone who doesn't mind acting like a doormat to others. If you are someone who stands on your ground and demands respect from those around you, you are likely to avoid being manipulated by people with bad intentions.

2. You are not afraid to express your opinions

If you're willing to express your opinions and explain your needs to others, you know that you're not going to get too far in life by refusing to speak up. When it comes to the manipulator, they keep away from anyone who isn't afraid to stick up for themselves. It shows that you can prioritize your needs and communicate in order to meet your needs.

3. You're not afraid to say no

Manipulators are looking for those who are afraid to say no. They aim purposefully at people who are willing to agree without asking too many questions. If you're not scared to tell someone you're uncomfortable with or just unwilling to agree with, chances are you're safe from those who want to use you to get ahead.

4. You set the sequences

A manipulator will test your boundaries to see how far you can be pushed. By setting boundaries and explaining the consequences of crossing the line, you demand respect and let people know that you cannot be manipulated.

5. You're using the time to your advantage

If someone is trying to manipulate you, they may require an immediate response or immediate action to put pressure on you. If you are able to use these moments to distance yourself from the manipulator and refuse to be intimidated, the manipulator will most likely return.

6. You are taking action

Manipulators target passive people because they're easier to control. If you set targets and take action, you're not likely to be the target. Knowing what you need and going after that will scare off the people who want to manipulate you.

7. You confront those who are trying to manipulate you

Manipulators are playing their game because they're good at it. In the past, they have had success in using people to get ahead. Being able to recognize someone who's trying to use you and being strong enough to stand up to them will stop a manipulator dead in their tracks. If you're willing to confront them, they won't be back in round two.

CONCLUSION

The vulnerability can work on multiple levels: if you're particularly happy with something , a manipulative individual will exploit your positive mind-set to persuade you to accomplish something you wouldn't typically do.

On the other hand, if you're crying and pouring your heart out to this person, you might be coddled and supported at the moment. But, somewhere down the line, when this person decides that they need something from you, they're going to remind you of what a "good friend" they were to you when you needed it. A manipulative person aims to control the people around them. Whenever anything hinders that process, you're likely to see that they're either emotionally or physically frustrated. They might react in an over-the-top way, perhaps with a huge temper tantrum. More often than not, however, a manipulative person communicates their frustrations in more subtle ways, such as giving you the cold shoulder.

Manipulative people can be absolutely furious in an argument or even in a healthy debate. They're the kind of individuals who, when they "respond" to something you just said, really just say whatever they want to say. You can tell that they're not actually listening to you in a meaningful way. Manipulative techniques are very advanced in today's modern world, and many people are emotionally manipulated and even persuaded to do what they don't do in their life practice. Mind-reading skills of an individual are needed to be able to identify emotional manipulators and influencers. As I promised in this book, you will learn the skills and techniques needed to get rid of being manipulated and handle them properly.